# Homes that Move

Heinemann
LIBRARY
Chicago, Illinois

To contact Capstone Global Library please phone
800-747-4992, or visit our website www.capstonepub.com

Edited by Daniel Nunn and Abby Colich
Designed by Cynthia Akiyoshi
Picture research by Mica Brancic
Production by Sophia Argyris
Originated by Capstone Global Library

ISBN 978-1-4329-8067-2 (hc)
978-1-4329-8072-6 (pb)

**Library of Congress Cataloging-in-Publication Data**
Smith, Sian.
  Homes that move / Sian Smith.
    pages cm.—(Where we live)
  Includes bibliographical references and index.
  ISBN 978-1-4329-8067-2 (hb)—ISBN 978-1-4329-
8072-6 (pb) 1. Dwellings—Juvenile literature. 2. Tents—
Juvenile literature. 3. Mobile homes—Juvenile literature. 4.
Houseboats—Juvenile literature. I. Title.
  GT172.S66 2014
  392.3'6—dc23                    2012046428

**Acknowledgments**
We would like to thank the following for permission to
reproduce photographs: Getty Images pp. 5 (Lonely Planet
Images/Jane Sweeney); 7 (Image Source); 8 (Robert Harding
World Imagery/C Gascoigne); 9 (AFP Photo/Anne-Christine
Poujoulat); 10 (The Image Bank/Alan Powdrill); 14 (Lonely
Planet Images/Scott Darsney); 15 (hemis.fr/Christophe
Boisvieux); 17, 23 top (Panoramic Images); 18, centre top
(Peter Arnold/Fred Bruemmer); 21 (Lonely Planet Images/
Doug McKinlay); Library of Congress pp. 12, 23 centre bottom
(Prints & Photographs Online Catalog); Shutterstock pp. 4, 22
bottom right (© Alexandra Lande); 6 (© Galyna Andrushko); 11
(© Baloncici); 16, 22 bottom left (© Tracing Tea); SuperStock
pp. 13 (National Geographic); 19, 22 top left (age fotostock/
Ton Koene ); 20, 22 top right, 23 bottom (The Irish Image
Collection).

Front cover photograph of a houseboat in Kerala, India,
reproduced with permission of Shutterstock (© Alexandra
Lande). Back cover photograph of nomads in the Kyrgyz
Republic reproduced with permission of Shutterstock
(© Tracing Tea).

Every effort has been made to contact copyright holders
of any material reproduced in this book. Any omissions will
be rectified in subsequent printings if notice is given to the
publisher.

# Contents

# Why Do Some Homes Move?

Some people live in homes that move.

Some people keep moving so their animals can find food.

Some people keep moving to sell things in different places.

Some people keep moving to see new places.

# Types of Moving Homes

Some people live on houseboats.

bed

Inside a houseboat there is a bedroom and bathroom. There is also a kitchen.

Some people live in homes on wheels.

Inside a mobile home, everything fits in a small space.

In the past, many people lived in tents.

Tents are easy to put up and take down.

# Tents Today

Some people live in tents today.

chum

Some people live in tents called chums. They move to find food for their reindeer.

yurt

Some people live in tents called yurts. Yurts can be made of wood and wool.

16

Bedouin tent

Some people live in tents in the desert. Tents in the desert give cover from the sun and wind.

# Changing Homes

igloo

blocks of snow

Sometimes people build a new
home each time they move.

Some people live in igloos in the winter and tents in the summer.

# Moving Together

Sometimes groups of people travel together.

Traveling as a group can help people stay happy and safe.

# Around the World

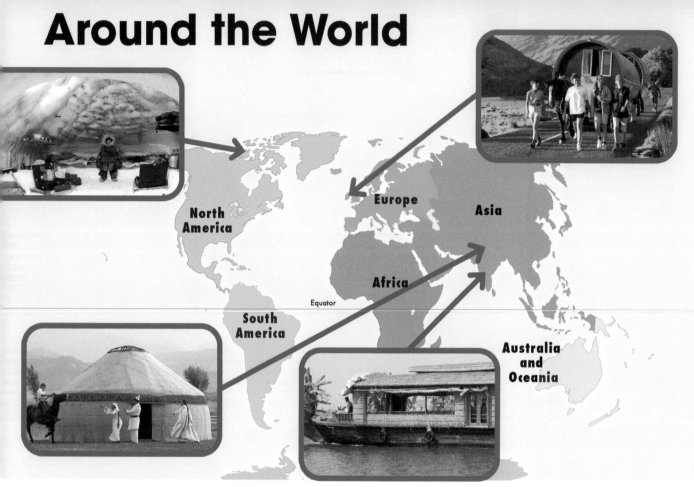

Follow the arrows to find out where each of these homes are found.

More information on page 24

# Picture Glossary

**desert** place that does not get much rain

**igloo** home made from blocks of snow

**tent** home made from poles covered with material

**travel** to move around and see new places

# Index

## Photograph information

The photographs in this book were taken at the following locations: p. 4 Kerala, India; p. 5 Turmi, Africa; p. 6 Daraw, Egypt; p. 7 United States; p. 8 Kashmir, India; p. 9 Marseille, France; p. 10 Florida, United States; p. 12 United States; p. 13 Russia; p. 14 Omnogov, Asia; p. 15 Khovsgol Province, Mongolia (chum is pronounced "choom"); p. 16 Kyrgyzstan; p. 17 Tunisia; p. 18 Canada; p. 19 Gojahaven, Canada; p. 20 County Mayo, Ireland; p. 21 Bamiyan, Afghanistan.

## Notes for parents and teachers

Look at the title of the book and brainstorm types of moving homes the children expect to find inside. Read the book together and discuss why people might need homes that can move. Compare the insides of different homes, for example the yurt (called a "ger" in Mongolia) on page 14 and the igloo on page 19. What do the two homes have in common? Discuss how homes provide us with a place to eat and sleep, and keep people and their things safe from the weather. Use the photograph information above to select a group of people to find out more about. Help the children to research the group and discuss the importance of community, traditions, and the feelings of belonging to part of a group.